Migrations

Poems

Lucy Dougall

For Dave Nosh + Pat,
dear friends of many
years + many adventures.
and misadventures!
with much love
from Lucy

iUniverse, Inc.
New York   Bloomington

Migrations

Cover Photo: Salmon Spawning in Bear Creek, Alaska; Niebrugge Images.
Cover Design: Pat Torpie, Alec Bay Graphics.

iUniverse books may be ordered through booksellers or by contacting:

iUniverse
1663 Liberty Drive
Bloomington, IN 47403
www.iuniverse.com
1-800-Authors (1-800-288-4677)

ISBN: 978-1-4401-0498-5 (pbk)
ISBN: 978-1-4401-0528-9 (ebk)

Printed in the United States of America

iUniverse rev. date: 11/22/2008

Migrations

Grateful acknowledgements are made to the editors of the following publications and competitions where some of these poems first appeared:

Love and Survival by Dean Ornish, "The Race"; Harp Strings Poetry Journal, "Ann's Stones"; Bellowing Ark, "Maiti Devi"; Friends Journal, "Invisible Bonds," "Tent in the Sky," "Mt. Stickney"; International Anthology of Little Press Poets, "Rift Fire"; The Lyric, "The Return"; New Hope International Review, "Tent in the Sky"; New Hope International, Positively Poetry, "Rift Fire"; PoetsWest Literary Journal, "Mt. Stickney," "Girl Island," "Rift Fire," "Tent in the Sky," "The Kiss," "Kidnapped"; Redwing Poetry Group Anthology, "Singing Stones," "Warnings," "The Return," "Next Generation"; North of Scotland Review, "Tent in the Sky"; Scottish International Open Poetry Competition Winners, "Edges, 2004," "Singing Stones, 2002," "Mt. Stickney, 2000."

Heartfelt thanks to my daughter, Sorrel North, for her ongoing encouragement and invaluable editorial assistance in assembling this collection; and to Tuie Sielicki and Mary Ann van der Meulen for their gracious participation in the final selection.

For my children, grandchildren,
and all those who come after.

Contents

EDGES

MIGRATIONS

Glamis Pictish Stone, 7th century. Glamis, Tayside, Scotland.

The Salmon of Wisdom is one of the oldest creatures in Celtic mythology. It is said to have acquired its great knowledge from eating the Nine Hazels of Wisdom that fell from the Tree of Knowledge into the Well of Wisdom. The ancient Celts and Picts believed that through eating the flesh of salmon one gained sacred knowledge from the Otherworld. Northwest Coast Native Americans also revered the salmon and believed they were actually supernatural people who enjoyed eternal life. The Salmon People lived in great houses under the sea and offered themselves to humans for food. Their spirits, in the form of bones, were then returned to the ocean where they were reborn. Because of the salmon's unique and amazing life story—hatched in freshwater rivers to journey hundreds of miles down to the sea, then years later migrating back to the exact place where they were born—these magnificent fish have come to symbolize the eternal cycle of life.

Invisible Bonds

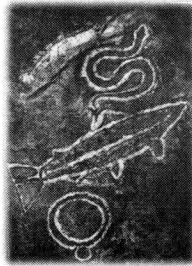

The Kiss

A Polish count
came up to me and
kissed my hand.

He told me that
my poem spoke
a language that he knew.

The surface broke,
a golden carp came
swimming through my heart.

Acacia Sunsets

Two chairs outside
a white mud hut,
two glasses of red wine.

We watch in silence
silhouettes of lace,
the thorn trees

cutting holes
in blood-red skies.
Sudden night drops

like a curtain
at play's end.
The ritual re-knits

us to the land,
to mysteries
and to each other.

The Race

A message burns the wires: he's had a heart attack.
My world goes black; blood plummets to my feet.
Just blocks away, the seven mile human ribbon ripples
lazily as thousands throng the streets of San Francisco
walking, jogging, joking, pushing prams. He made it
over Heartbreak Hill, past the Panhandle, into the Park
then fell. His heart stopped, full cardiac arrest, dead,
in any other time or place; but synchronicity, coincidence,
miracle or fate, whatever name we give to forces
that we cannot understand, gave him another chance.

If we lived back in ancient Greece where gods personify
these forces, ruling that one man should pay the price for pride,
another for neglect, perhaps Athena would have said
of him, *It's not his time. There is something he has left undone.*
In hours and days of waiting, I watch monitors and charts,
learning the foreign language of ischemia, infarction,
ventricular fibrillation, plaque and platelet—that stop
the flow of vital oxygen and blood.   But other nouns

and verbs can block the pathways to the heart: moments
of our lives we let slip by through inattentive fingers,
smug confidence that makes us feel invincible.
I walk the park where flowers assail me like battalions
of wild color, hyperboles of purple, rose, magenta,
vermilion, violet and gold. Life takes me by the neck
and shakes me hard, *wake up, it's right here all around you.*
This time Monet and Rumi send their messages to me.

Jane

Today is a blanket day, soft,
a light breeze, not too bright.
Wet wool does not like sun.

When asked about the weather
Jane usually answers
with a laconic, *Variable.* It suits
this Scottish island where
brilliant sun shape-shifts
to gales and rains inside a moment.

She knows the moods of Iona skies.
Cold is coming, you know,
when sky turns duck-egg blue.
In her long skirt, stout shoes,
home knit woolen cap, she's out
in any weather, feeding sheep
battling the wind to plant a garden,
making new gardens of beach stones.

Islanders fasten to their moorings
and endure, like sea pinks
on the planet-old stones.
Only the tough survive, Jane says,
I have lived here alone
and I know.

She welcomes you with tea and scones
and if you know her well,
Perhaps a wee dram? and, of course,
stories of her early days
when she left her island home in the north
in her blue coat. *I always had itchy feet and*
wanted to see what was over the next hill,
only to return, years later
to another island, another croft.

No matter what turns her life
takes, her salty humor buoys her.
That's just the way it was, she says.
Family names repeat themselves
among the living and on gravestones
where lie Jane's husband
and her only son.

She has finished mourning,
she strides across the island
gathering Greenstones and wild primroses
for her rock-walled garden by the sea.

Mt. Stickney

They did not come to climb the mountain,
hunt a deer or fall a tree. We saw them
where the snow still lingered, far up
the long rough logging road—
three older men in work clothes—
collars up, wool caps crusted with snow.
In a hollow near their truck, wind-sheltered
by snow banks, they crouched around a fire
cradling coffee mugs, feasting on sandwiches.
They motioned us to their circle.
One of them said, *We're three old friends.*
My father took me fishing up here as a kid.
I come each spring. I thought of my own father
and wished I had made for him so simple a memorial.

Two Women In Kathmandu

In a hotel in Kathmandu,
I meet a woman
turned back on the mountain
by accident and sudden sickness.

I stay at her bedside for three days
listening to her story, holding her hand.
Anguished and delirious, she pours it out -
a nightmare of the soul.

In a motel, in Pennsylvania, a friend
and I lie stretched out on beds
all day and night, both ill,
our hearts in critical condition,

laughing and remembering days of girlhood
and the rules we scorned together.
Unbroken confidences,
uninterrupted friendship.

There it is - as hard as bedrock,
deep as earth, the bond connecting
women's lives - rites of childbirth,
years of motherhood, a fierce devotion.

So many midnight conversations,
so much love,
sometimes with a complete stranger,
sometimes with your oldest friend.

Andy's Lake

was once a field of wheat
stippled by the sun.
Now flooded, it grows reeds,

lures water birds and moose,
shimmers with orange clouds
that float on its glassy surface
like orange melons.

Andy will lose a season's crop
but figures he has gained
a gift he could not plant.

Dody

Families disperse across the world
creating gain and loss. What
can replace the signals of the eyes,
a hand's touch or loved voice and
the body's quick unspoken messages?

How many times I wished that you were here
when you lived far from me, in Greece,
so we could talk away the afternoons
over our cups of tea or country walks,
then I would phone but it was not the same.

I flew to Switzerland when you were sick
that coldest winter in a hundred years
when swans froze in the ice-bound lake,
sat by your bed, read to you Tolstoy
then we went south for your recuperation

to Vienna. Its opera house glittered in the snow,
its chocolate pastries filled us with delight,
and we watched the Lipizzaner stallions dancing.
The cold pursued us further south to Rome
where wolves prowled in the city seeking food.

Then south to Naples in our last vain hunt
for warmth. Forty years later we went to Italy
again, to Florence, for three entrancing weeks.
We lodged in a student Pensione, talked, walked,
laughed, feasted, and found our spirits matched.

When speech and understanding left,
your body lived but all the rest had fled:
your keen intelligence and wit, your quick
grasp of a complicated thought, your love
of music, art, of flowers and good books.

Now I talk to you in my mind, see you
in gestures of another's hand or trip
on childhood memories that made us laugh.
I will not let the thread that binds us break;
you are somewhere, holding the other end.

Yna In Chile

Yna always wore pink—
pink jacket, pink dress,
pink kerchief, pink shoes,
high-heeled and glossy,
clicking on the cool cement.

Students whispered
not too kindly,
teachers speculated.
Why did she teach
year in year out?
She did not have to.

A spinster of good family,
a busybody, some thought,
always volunteering,
giving too much.

Tall, not really graceful,
steadfast as the Andes
high above the school,
she was tolerated.

Later on we discovered
she wore pink for him
who saw her as a rose
who asked her to wait,
but who never came.

Girl Island

Down the bank they plunge—
a caravan of women
carrying folding chairs,
mats, sun hats, books—
to where the river bends
and braids in channels
of green flashing water.

Wading to a stony island,
there they form their circle
a garland of wildflowers
on the sea-green violet
stones set around them
in the sand like bright
mosaics in a Moorish bath.

Mothers, daughters, sisters,
cousins, generations
mixing like a dough
that rises with the yeast
of strong affection, trust
as deep and steady
as the clear running river.

There they ask and answer
all the old translucent
questions about children,
lovers, families—bonds
that fray and break or mend
and heal. They could be
from any time or place,
at any well, on any shore.

When sounds of laughter
ring over rushing water
I will remember
the summer of Girl Island
though the stones may wash away
and the green and flashing waters
find new channels to the sea.

Home Birth

I rode the ferry north to the island that winter day.
Her house was neat, the little pile of infant clothes
all stitched by hand, clean, fragrant, near her bed,
embroidered with a pony and a rowan tree—
in Scotland, tree of magic power, of May garlands.
Rowan would be his name.

She lies propped up on pillows, face all inner joy,
and so begins our watch. Slow hours uncoil as day folds
into night. *Only one candle, so the light*
won't hurt his eyes, she says, *after his long warm*
months of darkness. We talk in whispers, walk
in stockinged feet, look at the clock, stoke up the stove.
The midwives take turns sleeping. I cannot sleep.
Our world is sealed inside this room. I relive births
of all our children, jump at each intake of breath.
Outside, nothing is real.

Can people still be feeding dogs and fighting wars?
The midwives take her vital signs, pace back and forth.
Contractions come in steady fire, no rest between
as hours drag by until the dawn. I lay cool cloths
across her brow, help her to sip, say words of comfort
while I feel her pain, a vise squeezing my gut.
A sudden rustling in the trees outside the window—
Rowan is riding in on the wind, his mother says.
Then finally an anguished cry, the head breaks free,
out shoots the dripping bundle slippery as a calf.
For one slow moment, all is peace.
They lay the baby in my daughter's waiting arms.
His breathing comes unevenly; they tend to him
while she sinks into shock, blood dark in pools beneath her.
Quick, phone emergency, help! *Let her not die.*
A car pulls up. Three medics burst into the room

inject IV, strap her and baby to a stretcher
lifting running carrying her like litter bearers
in a war across the rough and stubbled field toward
roaring just landed helicopter, blades still turning,
slide her through the open door and stand aside.

We watch it rise into the clear cold air.

Ann's Stones

Small universes hatch, sea-green like foam,
cool as the ocean floor, smooth to caress,
or ivory white of bleached whale bone,
offerings of grace intense as pangs of birth.
She chisels deep into the native stone,
follows the grain's strict inner map,
chipping flakes through jagged lines of fracture,
scraping with rasps then polishing with sand.

She sheds possessions gladly, her only room
spare as a winter beach; she keeps her books,
a few blue beads, blue china, dangling crystals
that crack the sun into bright shafts of fire.
The rounded breath that makes her whole
infuses life into the glowing stones.

Shiva Ratri

Tika powder—sacred, consecrating,
scarlet, crimson, carmine, saffron hued
heaped to gaudy craters on white sheeting
in the dusty streets of Kathmandu.

Courtyard of the temple, cindered confluence,
holy men cross-legged, steeped in prayer,
coated in white ashes, burning incense,
acrid, smoky fumes stifling the air.

Across India since time primeval
stream the pilgrims, devout teeming hordes
for the sacred night of great Lord Shiva,
of all deities the most adored.

We come of colder faiths, more monochrome,
yet feel their yearning spark and leap to flame.

Love

I will carry it with me
like the sound of the ocean
heard in a shell,

the memory of one sweet night
out in the pasture when you sang
our favorite song to me.

That song sung in a cracked voice
at our family circle around the fire
melted my heart

that song, and the red red rose
you grew yourself
and gave to me.

Next Generation

When children have grown up and gone their ways
door knobs aren't sticky and mud stays outside
where it belongs and those frenetic days
of rowdiness and recklessness subside
and give way to a hollow restful calm
like streets in Rio after Mardi Gras.

Then they come back with children of their own
in the trance of believing that their dramas
are all new, and so they are and you
can revel in their life at one remove,
spared vigils through the night, the suffering through
unending tests of will, deep disapproval,
slamming doors. All gives way to elation
and you are ready for the next generation.

Invisible Bonds

What have you done with the day, my dear,
what have you done?

Nothing much. Nothing much.
Wrote to some old friends,
encouraged a niece,

laughed with a grandchild,
took a walk in the fields,
dug weeds in the garden,

planned a family gathering,
phoned a far-away sister,
wrote a song.

The day has gone. What will remain?
Invisible bonds, invisible bonds.

Edges

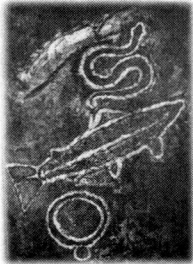

Drowning

It can happen. Life turns upside down
in a moment. I sat idly on the beach watching
my two small sons playing in the waves.
In the next moment we were all gulping salt water,

gasping for air. I had to tread water
and hold them up but a relentless undertow
kept pulling us out to sea
and then it happened

like a miracle. Out of the empty ocean
a boat appeared right next to us.
A young man and his father leaned over
and calmly pulled the boys aboard

and I swam back to shore.
Of course you should thank anyone
who saves the lives of your children.
Of course it is the least thing you can do

but I could not do it. Some things are so big
they cannot be said. And so I never thanked them
even though they were staying right across the street.
And I never saw them again.

Lake Isabel

I know it's up there. I've seen it on a map,
as clearly marked as a street sign.
The guidebook is tantalizing: *big and wild*
and blue beneath Ragged Ridge and
though the route is a bit confusing
the hiker who keeps his destination in mind
won't have trouble making the right choices.

We have read and reread about the forks,
switchbacks and boulder-beds, the crumbling
log bridges that cross the river,
the steep green tunnel up a ladderway
of roots skirting by inches a waterfall
and emerging finally into a forest of giant cedars
at the very outlet of the lake.

Our simple day hike has become a quest
and I wonder if we are not pure enough,
if merely searching for it time after time,
getting lost, benighted, black with mud,
bruised and scratched, worn out
by crawling under and climbing over
fallen trees lacing the steep slope,
drenched like mosses, is not enough.

I'm glad we have not found it,
that it still remains elusive,
that it may in fact have vanished in the mist
or have been put on the map by someone
who wanted to hold out to us
a beautiful, unreachable goal.

The Rabbi's Wife

She hobbled out of the synagogue and down the steps.
His chivalry stirred, he offered her his arm.

May I accompany you? he asked.
Yes, and I live across the town, she answered.

The journey was long and slow and his irritation mounted.
She did not seem bothered by his inconvenience,

that he would be late for his important appointment
because of an impulsive gesture.

When they finally arrived, she turned to him
with a parting word, *Always thank the Lord*

for putting someone in your way whom you can help.

For The First Time

I grew up with the ocean,
the wonder of waves breaking
again and then again upon the sand,
the changing colors—the indigo blue distance,
the gray-green nearness—the spindrift
and foam, the sound of pounding breakers,
the sizzling hiss of their grainy return.

I saw each day the vast unbounded
span of it interrupted, sometimes, far
far out by the mast of an infinitely
small fishing boat suspended
on the edge of water-sky.

My grandchildren have never seen
the ocean. They race with their mother
across the wide beach to the water.
Rowan shouts
Hurry, Mom, hurry, hurry
before they stop breaking!

and Callie
eyes wide in wonder, murmurs
These waves are so old
they come all the way from Africa.

A Sister's Story

Forebodings

We leave her in an airport inner room
behind a door of glass and separation.

Our mouths move soundlessly
like mouths of fishes, words

drowned in liquid walls
yet eyes connect and lock

a gaze that holds suspended
all our long life together.

My hand flies to my cheek
still warm from hers

she waves then turns and
merges slowly with the crowd.

Respite

Her life winds down into a five room
flat. The mind that once spanned
continents of music, politics

and art now focuses on medicines
and journeys down the hall. Days
snail along and hang like tentacles

of lead. But when I come from
half a world away, over our tea and
letters from the past, we tap the veins

of family memories, rocking
with laughter at those whirling days
when we were young, when life was

full of sound and fury, confusions
and cross purposes and, as she
loved to say, *chaos, as usual.*

Coma

What lies behind
those blank blue eyes that
stare unseeing into mine?
Only a year ago she had a life.

She moved, however haltingly,
we went for walks. She spoke,
listened to music, saw friends.
Does she feel trapped?

Does she feel anything?
She lies like a rag doll, limp
on the stiff hospital bed
without bone or muscle.

All we can bring are flowers
she cannot see or smell,
soothing hands she cannot feel
and voices she cannot hear.

To operate or not? We weigh
the risks. What would she choose?
Would she want to live on inside
an inert body and a shipwrecked mind?

Back Home

At first able to react to our rememberings,
she tells us stories through cacophanies
of senseless sounds——in a sort of desperation
clinging to them as to a life raft

in a sinking world, dispersing phrases
of assertion and command, even rare glints
of her old humor. Words come like sled dogs
tangled in their traces, with a sudden

Take me home! — this cry of sorrow
for the country of her childhood and
brief sparks of joy struck by the names
of a loved movie or a book, then days

of apathy and silence. But now,
caught in a tightening net, she is a lion
lashing out in spits and hisses,
her hands shaking the wheelchair

in frantic uselessness, her will not yet
extinguished inside her helpless body.
We sit politely and pretend she has not changed
though we are torn apart inside. We are

scavengers who snatch at lucid tidbits,
hoping to find an inner life
behind her troubled brain.
Are we watching a panther pacing

his cramped circles in the Paris zoo, seeing
only a thousand bars and behind that, nothing?
In our yearning to help are we, also,
imprisoned by a thousand bars?

Tucking Sheets

I tuck in line-fresh sheets
wind-tossed like fields of wheat

redolent of ocean salt,
smooth and taut

as sails in a stiff breeze.
Pillows puffed with down

from arctic geese perch
on blankets of sea blue.

Fragrance of flowers
permeates the bath

where fixtures gleam
like polished shells

immaculate and white.
These are my offerings

on Welcome's altar stone
where an open door

lets in the fresh wind
that can change your life.

Winter Lambing

At midnight on her knees among the sheep
she takes a scalpel to a lamb that died
and cuts its skin with infinite care to shape
a coat for a living orphan lamb in need
of a new mother. I watch but can't take part.

The meaning here is in the living, caring
for all of life, wherever it is sent,
forgetfulness of self and somehow bearing
with humor ancient rituals of a farm.

She lives in fundamentals, rhythm'd by seasons;
she cannot take a reckless chance or dream;
she answers to her heart's call, she has chosen.
I can't restart, begin where she began
nor will I fit into a new lamb's skin.

Warnings

High on the trail we break out
on an ancient gray moraine, inhale
cold thin air under lowering clouds
that hide the peak. Pitted volcanic
rocks mark the slope like Braille,
silent records of what lies beneath,
reminding us the mountain only sleeps.

Marmot sentries whistle alerts
from rock to rock, like bonfires
on the mountain tops signaling
the fall of Troy. Suddenly cold,
we watch the crystal beads floating
on lupine, blue as the chill wind.
For a dazzling moment, the scrim drops

as if waiting for our complete attention
to unmask the blinding white volcano
against a cobalt sky. Fumaroles
spew gases from a roiling center.
We hear or think we hear a muffled
rumbling warning us to leave.
The mountain dissolves again in mist.

Down in the dark silence of the forest
a ruffed grouse ruffles feathers,
branches skreak overhead, a bear
glides across our path, black fur
bristling. Her agate eyes burn
into ours. Perhaps she knows
we are standing on the Rim of Fire.

Tent In The Sky

One night, we staked our tent
on a high ridge after a long climb.
In darkness we found a site
wind-sheltered
by low fragrant pines.

I saw a brimming cauldron,
midnight blue, alive
with a million stars.
The dipper hung up among them
close to Polaris, at rest
after a day of scooping up
the stars and flinging them
wide into the night.

Some overflowed and fell
into distant pockets of the shore
where they became homes,
as welcoming as our yellow tent,
aglow with its single candle.

Johnny

He was one of the wild cousins.
Summers of childhood I haunted his barn,
bewitched by the sweet-sour reek of hay, manure,
foaming bridles; by the creak and shine of worn leather,
halters and harnesses, tack hung at random on old
wooden pegs, shelves stained dark as blood holding
English saddle soap, neatsfoot oil, bag balm and fly spray,
rusty rasps, hoof picks, bot knives, sweat scrapers,
curry combs, brushes, a clutter of ointments and salves
in mysterious small pots and jars. Like Merlin,
he charmed me into his kingdom.

Wiry, restless, all spring and sinew, grinning with mischief,
he pranced like a thoroughbred on legs faintly bowed
from a life in the saddle. *John, you thrive on action,*
his headmaster said, watching the boy score at football,
again and again, one eye closed, teeth loose, blood
pouring from nose, mouth and ears. Horses possessed him,
provided they were fast, wild and—preferably—unbroken.

The mania started with Little Suzanne, a two-year-old
racehorse, *a steal,* Johnny said, *why, look at her papers,*
she'll make me a fortune, but that's not what lured him.
It was all in the game: buying and selling, outwitting,
out-talking. As for training, his mode was free-wheeling,
no coaxing, cajoling or gentling for him; in certain
tough cases, he told me—though I never saw it—
he had to resort to direct application of a stout two-by-four.

Johnny moved to Ireland taking his wild, reckless youth
into wild, reckless old age. Though tempted by any
mad scheme or rash venture, you could not fool Johnny.
He swallowed books whole and never forgot a word.
Nor was he backward at setting people straight. In his
hundreds of letters to the Irish Times he blasted bigotry,
terrorism, IRA priests, the whole educational system
and whatever else came to mind. *Oh, so you are the Mr. Bond*
who writes all those letters, people would say, *I've always*
wanted to know what you looked like.

On he went, breaking horses, riding, dancing, even fox-hunting
into his seventies, jumping with foolhardy abandon. Once
he collided on top of a stone wall with some other huntsman
sending both men and their hearing aids, false teeth and glasses
flying to the winds, enjoying every minute of it. People like Johnny shouldn't
get old or get emphysema. To him life was not worth living if he could not
be John Bond, all out for life. So one day,
he went out to his barn with a shotgun
and shot himself.

The Field of Light

The mind is a many-storied house
the breathing archives of our lives –
memories stored in rooms

that spill into annexes and sheds,
barns, chicken coops and orchards,
into woods and countrysides.

Not neatly charted but unlocked at once
by a stray key – an image, scent or sound.
A sudden whiff of new cut hay,

the honeyed scent of summer
flings me back to childhood
riding horseback down a country lane.

Alone and innocent, I spied a field,
golden and shimmering, and no path led there.
Like a mirage in the desert

of longed-for water, it lured me on.
All summer, I retraced the ride but the field
had gone forever and ever since

I ponder why that image burned
so deep and keeps returning
across all the years

like a wildflower of the soul.

Atlantic Night

A woman's thin nightgown has washed ashore.
I lie in bed and listen to the northeast wind hammer
the banging shutters as thunder crackles down the walls.
Stories pitch and toss around my head to match the storm.
In the room below the grownups are still dining.
Voices rise and fall, break into laughter. Glasses clink.
A siren wails. The phone rings: *Shipwreck up the beach!*
I hear chairs scrape from tables, cars speed off.
The next morning, gray with acrid smoke, reveals
a pleasure ship, still smoldering, orange life jackets
strewn along the sand and one cold body of a woman.
She's so young. The grownups stand in silence.
I feel numb and old as I look on death for the first time.

Edges

Born in the sea
vanishing in the mist
islands have fluid edges
changing with the tides
places where the layer is thin
between what is known and what is not
between the land and sea
where waves roll in and out leaving
their cloud reflections on the sand
leaving a surface that seems solid
but is soft and yielding, taking
but not keeping footprints
in its myriad grains of sand.

Between the earth and sky
the green flash comes and goes
in heaven's blink. And in the rolling
fields of wheat the grain unsnaps
in a golden flash, as sudden
as the flame of sunset quenched
in the black of an African night.
A thin place cracks open
like a window in the sky
And wild geese cry out overhead
filling you with wild, irrational joy.

Migrations

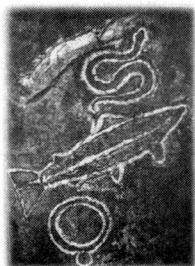

to Dave Nash & Pat
Greetings from Mt. Blanc
& Lake Annecy nearby where
we returned last summer
to celebrate our 60th
anniversary where it all began!
Much love   Lucy & Bill

Maiti Devi

The elephant is tied up next to my bicycle
contentedly munching at a large stack of hay.
He appeared suddenly last week,
led or ridden by his small master
over all those mountains
from India, to the south.

The pilgrim did not act as though
this were anything special,
just a journey of several hundred miles
over mountains
on an elephant.
He was coming to the festival of Shiva Ratri
to pay his respects
to the god.

Naturally, he tied up the elephant near a temple,
our little temple of Maiti Devi,
the gilt-roofed temple
with the green metallic birds, one at each corner,
poised to take flight,
the temple guarded by four mild lions
and three peacocks.

We, also, will go to the festival of Shiva Ratri.
But we are outsiders, looking in.
I feel friendly toward that pilgrim.
One day, I wake up and look out.
Maiti Devi seems strangely empty.
Where are the hay and the elephant?

People keep on walking, walking
slowly around the little temple.
An acrid smell of smoke wafts over
from the burning bodies on the ghats.
The hot sun beats down relentlessly on the dusty city.

I would not mind having
the kind of faith it takes
to ride an elephant over the mountains
for days and days
and miles and miles.

Grand Central Station At Midnight

On New Year's Eve the lofty concourse
echoes like a cathedral,
becomes a ballroom with an orchestra

playing waltzes. Strangers flock to the music
link arms in one long sinuous line,
to the universal language of the dance,

contracting and expanding
like an exuberant caterpillar
on its way to transformation.

I watch it from a balcony and think
this one brief moment may be enough to last
a whole lifetime, in someone's heart.

Picnic Passion

On the subject of picnics
I go along with Dickens
who made a ceremony or a drama
of almost anything, including picnics.

He walked twelve miles a day,
preferring the open air to—as he put it—
a perpetual simmering in hot rooms.
Outside, anything can happen:

a zebra migration can thunder by,
or two explorers looking for the source
of the Nile. A picnic is a celebration
whether by the side of the road

when the bus stops or standing
on a mountain trail in mid-winter
stamping your feet to keep warm.
It all goes back to an ancient time

when life turned on the seasons,
when the elements were elemental,
when twilight sealed the day
and the stars mattered.

Just being outside and being awake
can open doors to what's inside,
like the curtain going up on a play
that has yet to be written.

Kidnapped

Puffs of gaily colored cloth
loaf across an August sky,
turbans of hot air riding the wind,
remote as nebulae, until one sunset—

There's a balloon in our pasture!
shriek the children, scurrying
over meadows, pitching headlong
into ditches like tipsy rabbits,
racing toward the giant

scarlet toadstool. A basket
dangles underneath, now circled
by the wildly dancing children.
Come aboard, the captain beckons,
waving them into his wicker aerie.

They clamber over with whoops
and shouts, legs flailing.
The dragon snorts short fiery blasts,
hoarse orange flames belch forth
flooding the balloon with light

as it lifts slowly off the ground, trailing
its gondola of children above the treetops,
to become another chip of light
in the night sky to three astonished dogs
barking circles in the field far below.

What On Earth

Branches vault and arch
across the lane to form
a leaf-lined tunnel to our house.

Strange plants spring up,
field grasses reach to towering heights,
brambles spin walls of green barbed wire

that tangle me in tentacles of steel.
I hack and chop my way
with loppers, clippers, axe and saw.

The ice cap is melting,
a tropical jungle is on the march,
the equator is moving

north.

Rift Fire

Three green land rovers
churn through the African bush
like an ancient caravan
of camels. A red dust wake
spews into shining air
and dissipates. We stop
to camp in a clearing.
Tents rear up, sleeping bags
unroll, pots clatter.

Over the Great Rift Valley,
weightless clouds turn
violet then vermilion,
like gaudy spinnakers
before the wind.
Acacia trees, flat
as clotheslines, make
black cut-outs against
a sky of orange flame.
Birds fall silent
as darkness drops
with a soft thud.

We light the fire.
Twigs and dry leaves crackle,
spraying incandescent
arrows into the black.
The hoarse rasp of a distant
lion, rows of disembodied
eyes that gleam dull red
then vanish, send ancestral
shudders through us.
Arms shake the shadows
for wood to feed the blaze.
Did others sing, as we do,
to hold back the dark?

Velella Velella

Stranded fleets of jellyfish line the dark sands
of the shore like strings of blue glass beads.

Some call them blue bottles, Sailors-by-the-Wind,
for their cobalt hulls, for their crystal sails

set and trimmed to catch the winds on their Coriolus course
roaring clockwise around the wide Pacific.

Some unrecorded storm in mid-ocean roiled
up waves and currents tossing hulls by hundreds

on the California beach. There they lie shipwrecked,
their royal color fading, forgotten by the main flotilla

still sailing on the deepest ocean.

Rendezvous In Bangkok

Monsoon rains slap the windshield, headlights
flare like supernovas as we streak down strange
roads to a strange city. Disembarking in a torrent,
we wade into the hotel through fronds of floating
palms. Wood ceiling fans spin desultory circles
casting shadows through the cavernous lobby.
Scattered rattan chairs sag limply like old clothes hampers.
Morning brings the heat, the ring of temple bells
and our first pagodas—temples of tiered roofs,
steep-gabled, light as birds in flight, topped
by glittering, golden spires. Our window overlooks

an unkempt garden with a swimming pool.
Across a small table, two men lean toward each other
consumed in conversation. One is older,
an Englishman—nervous, smoking, rumpled
and seedy as the hotel—the other, a young Thai,
dark and vaguely raffish. Is it an assignation?
Some political intrigue? Perhaps their lives depend
on this last meeting. The Graham Greene plots
spin on inside my head. Outside, the street

is carpeted with seated vendors, cross-legged
under lampshade hats. Our way weaves
through oceans of salt fish, spiced rice, nose-stinging
curries and fruits arrayed as though for sacrifice,
cut open to their juicy hearts, small hedgehogs
of red prickles, green armadillos rank and succulent
swathed in bristling thorns. We return to the hotel
to savor our exotic catch. In the garden,
the men still sit—in silence now—caressing
their tall iced glasses, enfolded in their story.
Suddenly they rise, their faces masked,
impassive. Each goes his separate way.
And the temple bells keep ringing.

Singing Stones

Born in veins of rock
beneath the sea or
sluiced down rivers
from the far off mountains
cracked into fragments
tumbled by the pounding
waves, they come to rest
at last upon the sand.

The gray-green-violet pebbles
seem like pieces of the sky
carved out, cast down
to earth as glistening mosaics
renewed and polished
with each surging wave.

I fill my pockets full
to overflowing
then pour them out
around my inland home
so I can walk upon
the singing stones
and shut my eyes
and hear the sea.

Sand Painting

An old man kneels in a street of Kathmandu,
fingers flickering like candles in the niche
by the little temple. He leans back, weary, to view
his work of many days, a painting which
he drew in a palette of many-colored sands:
Buddha under his Bo tree, caught with an art
that flames to life in blazing golden strands.

He carries the reverent offering of his heart
to the sacred Bagmati river to submerge
the bright ephemeral image. With sudden force
it sinks through the cool waters, a mirage,
a shimmering of sand returning to its source.
He sifts it through his fingers like a dream
and watching it go, his wrinkled face beams.

Broken Willow

I watch my small son inch along
like a caterpillar on the crusty bark
of the willow tree that hangs
over the dark flowing stream,
wriggling in precarious balance, pulling
the almost too heavy rope. Then he ties it
with his boy scout knot, legs wrapped
round the branch like curving stems
while I stand far below holding my breath.

Is he thinking of Tarzan in darkest
Africa, outwitting tribes of cannibals
with their poisoned darts and sleek
pirhanas snapping near the banks?
At last the knot secure, he slithers back
and down until his feet land on a lower spur
and reaching high his hands along the rope
he leans far out and swings in a mighty arc
on jungle vines into a boy's dream.

A generation passes, then another
of swinging, twirling, shouting children,
flashing by like ripples on the water.
Today with a dry snap and crunching thud
it broke, that old willow branch
over the dark stream that flows along
as though nothing has changed.

Icebound In La Conte Bay

We have paddled for miles and for days
then the river pours into the sea
where our canoes glide
silently until we turn into the bay
and strike the first ice cakes
clinking together like wind chimes.

Flakes thicken into floes, nuzzle
our boat like porpoises and block
our way. Wind-driven blocks collide,
buckle and scrape the gunnels.
We stab our paddles at their turquoise

waterlines to fend them off.
Icebergs loom out of the mist
like stray ships. Calved from glaciers
they shear off in thundering hulks,
plunge deep into the bay to reappear

like sea monsters on an antique map.
At any instant they could somersault
and flip us over into the cold Alaskan
sea. We are trapped by the wind
in a vast floating museum of ice

carved and chiseled in crystalline
precision. The bay glitters pink and orange.
Caught in the crack between fear
and delight, we wait, and gamble
on a turning of the wind.

The Return

Waiting, pacing, ricocheting back
and forth, jumping at the phone's shrill ring,
watching hard for headlights through the black,
I conjure up disasters in a string
and calculate, as nervous stomach churns,
how long it takes to get you down the mountain/
down the river/ from the sky/ to then return
over the long miles home to where I wait.
Lights finally flare from darkness, brakes glissade,
the car door slams and you at last appear
smiling, unshaven, tired but flushed and glad,
laden down with pack and sopping gear.
The weight lifts from my heart, all knots untwine;
you leave your virile world and reenter mine.

Migrations

They have come back
children and grandchildren,
like eels born in the Sargasso Sea,

small translucent jellies
riding the Gulf Stream
of the wide Atlantic

back to their native waters
in a Scottish loch.
And ours too come back

for months or even years
to give to us the lavish present
of their youth, then leave again

to chart their own course
through the wide and unknown
ocean of their lives.

Printed in the United States
131659LV00009B/1/P